cherry cola
poems + essays

erica gerald mason

Sèvres Babylone
USA

© 2015, Erica Gerald Mason; all rights reserved. Cover photo by boule1301, DollarPhotoClub.

No part of this book may be used or performed without express written consent from the author, with an exception for critical articles and reviews.

To contact the author, send an email to hello@ericageraldmason.com

www.ericageraldmason.com

table of contents
- a smile made of flowers
- peaches
- adornment
- time
- food

a smile made of flowers

with a simple structure seventeen
syllables -written in three lines of five,
seven, and five, syllables - haiku is
poetry at it's most bare. poetry at it's
most elegant.

I.

thank you for reading
a haiku about haiku
yes, it's absurd.

II

but absurd or not
emotions are laid bare in

this simple format.

III

love, hope and longing
universal emotions
don't need many words.

1

she kept her heartache
on a hook, displayed like art
in a museum

2

those tears in your eyes
after all those silences -
those tears are mine now.

3

night then morning
i used to stay up to see
the sun; now i sleep.

4

i talk too much when
i'm nervous and too quiet
when happy - it's weird

5

when the sun rises
i turn over - pull you close
bargain for more sleep

6

not yet afternoon
but not morning anymore
i feel the sun shine

7

shadow follows me
she follows me everywhere
only wants to love me

8

i see and i hear
the wind move through the tall trees
louder every day

9

i love you the way
i love cherry cola - you're
so damn addicting.

10

my turn ons are small
smiles and big hearts with a side
of huge intellect

11

most warriors i
know became strong from battles
fought from the inside.

12

i used to smirk at
standing ovations but now
i stand up and cheer.

13

my cherry cola
has a thin lemon slice on
top. it floats, then sinks.

14

i sat on a bench
in Capri and thought about
a boy in Georgia.

15

i was never the
girl who was rolled in sugar
and dipped in sprinkles.

16

the flowers match my
mood but not my overall
sense of wellbeing.

17

you're so beautiful
when you have no idea just
how lovely you are.

18

sunday afternoons
when we have nowhere to be
you, me. perfect. free.

19

my first grown up drink
a brandy alexander -
tried once. no thank you.

20

black forest cake with
cherries soaked in rum - eaten
with the one you love

21

when you stand in front
of an unknown door, i hope
you will open it

22

even in the fog
surrounded by gray, you see
what shines, what shimmers.

23

the scent of figs is
enough to make me leave
this lovely corner

24

i want you to be
happy, so i write poems.
well. is it working?

25

we fall in love the
way we enter a pool - jump
in, ease in, pushed in.

26

head in the clouds, heart
not far behind. spread those wings,
believe you can fly.

27

i used to keep my
fears in a bottle. now i
sip them like soda.

28

when i accepted
my battle scars, i became
a true warrior.

29

lunch with your friends
arrive in blue and a half smile.
they all knew better.

30

this road may lead to
paradise or to ruin
but i'll enjoy the ride.

31

dear brave warrior
stop fighting the eternal
war within yourself.

32

the stars shimmer with
jealousy at how you can
shine without darkness.

33

the adventure is
in hoping daring loving
on this long journey

34

lifestyles are like shoes
some fit, others don't. you wear
your shoes, i'll wear mine.

35

i dabbed a slick of
red cherry cola lip balm
on my lips...taste me.

36

the brightest stars walk
you home and the stalwart moon
keeps watch til morning.

37

will you remember me?
the one who sat next to you
and smiled at your smile.

38

i am the only
one who can walk this lonely
road. you can't stay here.

39

the hibiscus tea
stains my lips a dark red. a
smile made of flowers.

40

i dream i'm floating
above the clouds below the
stars. a swirl of blue.

41

i love blueberries
in a white ceramic bowl
and filled to the top.

42

the wind in my hair
sun in my face radio
turned way up. summer.

43

i sat next to you
knowing i would be the last
one to hold your hand.

44

I.

i bought four plums but
only ate one. the others
became too moldy.

II.

i bought more plums so
i could have a tiny taste
of sweetness and light

III.

the plums were so sweet,
like fresh honey, but i thought
of fruit not tasted

47

just before the rain
the wind changes direction
the leaves dance and sway

48

how to fall in love:
take all your expectations
and put them away.

49

the only things i
know how to say in russian:
hello and thank you

50

my niece loves to hop
because she's four and she can
and it makes her glad.

51

the air at the top
of the volcano was cold
but the ground was hot.

52

i burned the toast but
we scraped off charred bits of bread
and ate what remained.

53

i'll have to leave you
someday - i won't know when - so
love me while you can.

54

all i need is a
quiet corner, a book. and
maybe some iced tea.

55

my favorite cup
has a chip at the rim. i
better be careful.

56

the wind blows. pink
petals fall from the tree like
cotton candy rain.

57

a wintery walk
a glimpse of yellow string.
you'll take it with you.

58

edge of the island
away from the lights, the sky
parts. stars dance in time.

59

talk talk talk more talk
words without sense or meaning
silence is golden

60

vanilla ice cream
with rhubarb and strawberry
sauce on summer nights.

61

the moonbeams dance and
glide along my ceiling. dreams
must wait patiently.

62

the wildflowers in
mason jar tempt the bees -
an insect brothel.

63

i use a sharp knife
to slice mushrooms and carrots
- a meditation.

64

a trench coat, cinched tight
protects from the wind and rain
outside, not inside.

65

this paper boat made
from magazine pages, tied
with purple string... floats.

66

darkened theater
cellphones glow. lighthouses, but
no rescue needed

67

the chairlift over
a ski resort without snow
keeps watch and still turns.

68

the Chinese lanterns
carried our hopes to the stars.
became one of them.

69

japanese maples
turn fiery red in fall
fire without flame.

70

the only time i'm
alone is in a crowded
room of so-called friends.

71

tell me i'm wrong or
tell me i'm right. but please care
enough to tell me.

72

I.
beyoncé is a
modern cleopatra but
baby, so are you.

II.

the same nice things
you say about beyoncé?
say about yourself.

III.

you seem to defend
beyoncé even more than you
stand up yourself.

75

watching idris in
luther is the best way to
spend the night, hands down.

76

the fortune cookie
factory is a place filled
with unwished wishes.

77

i draw a heart on
a foggy window for the
next person to see.

78

i wear purple when
i'm happy, blue when i'm not.
pink - never. at all.

79

hang your smile next to
the moon, you'll see it matches
perfect alignment.

80

the flowers you sent
lasted longer than we did
and began to bloom.

81

at midnight, the sea
twinkles with silver dust and
metallic mischief.

82

meet me at the park
the bench near the old fountain
i'll wait for you there.

83

the sun rises through
my window - pauses for me
to say 'good morning'.

84

i sleep and i sleep
but i don't dream of you so
i sleep and i sleep.

85

birdseed in each hand,
we wait for the bride and groom
outside of the church.

86

do you really want
a filtered processed faded
instagram-like life?

87

the scariest films
are ghost stories, with demons
you never quite see.

88

as i slept, spring left.
summer took it's place at dawn
with a lightning flash.

89

i wait in quiet
for the smallest sign of life.
anything will do.

90

would you rather be
only flower in the field?
or one of many?

91

in this small canoe,
i can make room for us both…
if that's what you want.

92

in my heart, there are
hallways lined with locked doors. you
have the only key.

93

i hung upside-down
on the monkey bars and laughed
at the mixed up world.

94

radio songs - words
i sang as a child, without
knowing what they meant.

95

i waited all day
for the sun, but it never
came to my window.

96

i wrote a poem
for you, but i thought you might
not like it. do you?

97

the soles of my shoes
are loose, making a thwack thwack
sound as I walk by.

98

new year's eve champagne
takeout thai and pajamas
party of the year.

99

the parade lasted
too long - we became bored of
cheering. smiled instead.

100

the sandwich maker
closed up shop after he sliced
the turkey and rye.

101

i've apologized
through gritted teeth. and i've said
f*ck you with a smile.

102

i'm too sensible
for fantasies - but i look
at the moon and sigh.

103

practical dreamers
look at stars and wonder how
the twinkle is made.

104

like a child who sees
snow for the first time, i saw
you and was speechless.

105

i want to wake up
in a wes anderson film
poised, placed, perfectly.

106

dinner for one at
at a table for two. alone
but not lonely. no.

107

prosecco, maybe.
champagne, of course. moscato?
i just want bubbles.

108

stale bubblegum in
a mouth too bored to chew. no
flavor to speak of.

peaches

it begins with a filtered photo of peaches
on Instagram
blurry high contrast balls of orange and
red
tempt me
taunts me
begs me to try
just one

delivery of Georgia peaches
the caption says
a glance at the account
shows me
the user lives
in Indiana
in my old town, actually
hi Bloomington

I've missed you think of you fondly do you
miss me?
there is a business which
delivers our Georgia peaches
to your town or
to your door
the peaches were in Bloomington the city where
I met fell in love with married
my husband
the city where I arrived a girl and left a
grown up a wife a mother
the peaches ended up where I began

Georgia peaches in Indiana
I'm an Indiana girl
now a Georgia woman
lived here for 15 years

it's been a long while since I've had a
good peach
a real peach
I'll get some peaches
right now
right this second

I'll walk
a beautiful day
lemon drop sun
and marshmallow clouds
the grocery store is just
a half mile away
put the two dogs away
Piper and Hero
the senior citizen and the young
ingenue

the springer spaniel and
the yorkie poo
the ambassador and the trouble starter

they've broken windows and doors
charging the door to greet
visitors delivery men
jehovah's witnesses neighborhood kids
selling cookies
so they go to their room
when I leave
tucked in and away
dogs out of sight
out of mind
not out of earshot
their barks say goodbye
and wish me a speedy return

I'm still in the driveway
when I realize
walking to the grocery store
is a terrible idea
in season Georgia peaches
mean in season
heat humidity sweat
misery

I'm determined
the most stubborn person
you'll ever meet
I want a peach
and I'll walk to get it
down the hill up the hill
the hill where during the

snowstorm of '14
cars trucks even the schoolbus
couldn't make it up the incline
so the drivers left vehicles
up and down the steep slope
an obstacle course of steel and rubber
today the course is clear

just me the road and the heat
walking down is a piece of cake
a hot fresh from the oven cake
two more rolling hills
up down up down
past the empty golf course
too hot to play

past the 4 way stop sign where
everyone stops

in every direction
each car too polite to be first
so I just wave and keep walking
past the lake
the new vet's office
the tiny but busy post office
finally the grocery store
a reprieve of cool air

the grocery store is **my** store
I know almost everyone
behind the counter
stocking the shelves
at the register
and almost everyone knows me
hey they say
everyone says hey in the south
and because I live
in the south now

I say hey, too

can I help you find something
I hear
once twice then three times
from passing employees
just getting some peaches
I say and wave hello
as I pass by

walk through the main aisle
glance at the paper towels
pause in the wine aisle
a cold apple cider sounds tasty
then remember my purpose
square my shoulders
and walk to the fruits and vegetables

Georgia peaches 99 cents a pound
I read
the display is beautiful
mounds flats bags
even pyramids
of peaches
I reach into my pants pocket
for my phone to take my own
photo of fresh Georgia peaches

no phone
no problem
no pictures
I'll buy the peaches
and bring them home
snap some photos at the kitchen counter
and everyone will know I can have
fresh Georgia peaches

any time I want
as long as it's summer time

I lightly touch one peach then two
then quickly squeeze
three four five six seven
eight nine
peaches
all hard as a rock
the fuzzy fruit has no give
no promise of a soft bite
or a melt in my mouth sensation

the peaches feel as if
somewhere
in the back of the store

there is a band of grocery workers
spray painting tennis balls
orange and red
then attaching tiny little
plu stickers to the sides
maybe adding mini branches to
every 8th one for effect

I'm feeling up all of the peaches
none are ready to eat
hey I hear
so I say hey
and turn around
it's one of the produce department
workers

long time no see I say
how are you

because in the south it's
not polite
to jump into business
without exchanging
pleasantries first
oh I'm fine he says just fine
and you
I'm good I say what's up with the
peaches
I ask
hard as a rock

I know he says
not ready yet
just put 'em in a paper bag for a few days
ripen 'em up
sounds good I say
but I wanted to eat them now
can't he laughs
my uncle grows peaches and he says

we send all the best peaches out of
Georgia
because everyone knows Georgia
peaches
are the best peaches
in the world

but what about the people who *live*
in Georgia I ask
what are we supposed to eat
I didn't ask my uncle that he says
paper bag two days ripen 'em
right up he says
see ya
see ya I say
back to work for him
while I find my Georgia peaches

I feel for three peaches
find the first one two
right away
but skip the next three
then find
the last fuzzy peach
near the top of a pyramid
next to a plum someone
placed in the pile
one of these things
is not like
the other

pay in cool air
walk home in hot air
down the hill
up the hill down
the hill up the hill
home

a shower a change of clothes
humidity means a
wardrobe change
a glass of cherry cola
then three yellow Georgia peaches go
into
a brown paper bag
for a two day nap

time passes quickly and
brown paper bags
fade into the background
so easily
two days turn to four

in the kitchen
the fifth morning

making a glass of iced tea
I notice the bag
reach for it
paper rustling
bag open
you know those
stores in the mall
those stores which sell scented candles
fragranced body lotions perfumed body
sprays
opening the bag is like walking into
that store
overcome with
the smell of Georgia peaches
the fragrance overtakes me
technical knock out
down for the count

the iced tea forgotten

I pick up the now soft peaches
ready to eat
miracle of transformation
hard turned soft
wash two of the peaches
leave one in the bag
the fuzz fighting the water
at first
then accepting it

a Georgia peach in each hand
a quick calculation
which one to eat first
the left has more of a reddish hue
like a stormy sunset
that's the one

lean over the sink

bound to be juicy
lick the peach first
something I can only do at home
the sensation of fuzz on the skin
is unlike any other fruit skin
I've ever eaten

open wide to bite
doorbell rings
dogs bark charge
say hello to the contestant
behind door number one

a sigh a shrug
peaches on kitchen counter
wipe hands on pants
grab the collar of the big one
scoop up the little one

special delivery
sign right here
please
van disappears
dogs retreat
I'm intrigued by this package

tape's too tight
this baby's not budging
better take it upstairs
use scissors in office
up the stairs
shaking rattling testing the box
in my office
at my childhood desk
open the drawer
purple scissors with black
duct tape on handles
one snip two snips

rip open the rest
gleaming black headphones

who ordered headphones
remember husband had
extensive conversation
about these very headphones
text husband
headphones here
quick reply
awesome with three
exclamation points
I'm happy he's happy

scissors back in desk
headphones on his side of the bed
back downstairs

to my Georgia peaches

the counter is clear
nothing remains
except puddles of water
clustered together in a Rorschach test
(a disheveled nest of four baby birds)
have I imagined the peaches
the smell
the slick of water on their skins
the feel of the peach on my tongue
I must have left the peaches on the table
not the counter
a glance at the table
tells me
I'm wrong
no peaches there

I walk toward the front door
retracing my steps
my dogs walk toward me
tiptoeing and not meeting my eye
the walk of the guilty
turn the corner and see it
two perfect peach pits
one right by the front door
the other on the bottom step

not a shred of peach flesh remains
I could plant the stones
right now
in the backyard
and in six years we'd have peaches
I pivot turn
Piper Hero
get over here
the dogs approach

guilty but not scared

dammit they even smell
like peaches
I tell them they are
bad bad dogs
but I pet them too
so I'm definitely sending
mixed messages
they are sent to
doggy timeout which is
what they normally do
which is lay on the couch
but instead of me sitting with them
I sit at the table
which doesn't seem to bother them
because they enjoy napping
and they just ate

I write a bit
while the dogs are in exhile
forget the peaches
forget the dogs in timeout
forget the headphones
forget everything the Instagram photo
forget the Georgia peaches
day passes into evening
which becomes morning

take two
let's try this again
a perfect Georgia peach for breakfast
that's gonna hit the spot
nothing on the counter
dogs don't look guilty
or smell like fruit
look up down around
inside next to

confounded and confused
call text Facebook husband
where's my Georgia peach
husband is remarkably understanding
considering I am bothering him at work
he knows nothing about peaches
my Georgia peaches
wishes me luck
I have no luck
no peaches
I settle for a peanut butter and
strawberry jelly sandwich

daughter awakens
hugs greetings
summertime ritual
swim library lunch home
read write games or tv until dinner
around the table

conversation laughter plans made
talk turns to grocery shopping
I lament my lost Georgia peach
Oh I ate that peach in the bag
I ate that last night for a snack
daughter says
silence

that was my peach
I say and realize how crazy it sounds
I'm pouting because someone ate my peach
my Georgia peach
I rally recover regroup
I say
tell me how it tasted
how it felt as you ate it
explain it to me
a shrug a squint a furrowed brow

I don't know
she says
it tasted like a peach
it was really good and sweet
I laugh and I say
it's funny

it's really funny
I was going to write about those Georgia
peaches
I thought there was a poem in there,
somewhere
was there
I ask her
was there a poem
in those peaches
I don't know
she says I don't know about

these things

so I tell her
I tell her how what we taste isn't just
hot sweet salty or spicy
it's smell sound texture temperature
beauty fanciness and how we eat it
she listens intently nodding
every now and again
and then she says
it was just good
I don't know how else to say it

days pass a week
then two
I've forgotten about Georgia peaches
and how
I almost had three

a phone call
my mother is going to a casino in
Alabama
for a few days
do I want to come along
even though I don't gamble
sure a mini break
is just what I need

so I pack my bags
let's go to Alabama
casino bound
four hours to fun
we sing laugh talk
talk about family friends
and Georgia peaches
we laugh about luck timing
say it's funny how these things happen
because it is funny

we make good time
here's our exit
off the highway and make a left
I can see the casino
there off the highway
in Alabama
side roads
almost there
pass a the gas station parking lot
where a man
with a cooler
and a sign
which says
Georgia peaches for sale
look I say
and do a little dance in my seat
I'm going on an adventure
after dinner

check in bags unpacked dinner's done
mom's off gambling
I'm on my own
night is speeding towards the hotel
time for some Georgia peaches
the gas station is further than I thought
on foot

a 5 minute stroll
is actually a 20 minute walk
no sidewalks
along a highway
starting to have my doubts
when I'm there

the man selling peaches
is elderly
short white hair short sleeved white
shirt
khaki shorts white shoes
sitting in a folding chair
hey he says
oh hey I say
I saw your sign for fresh Georgia
peaches
yep he says got them right here
he opens the cooler
where'd you get them I ask
just got back from Florida
he yawns
picked some up on the way home
thought I could make a few bucks
I'm from Georgia
I say a Georgia girl in Alabama

buying Georgia peaches
but
he's instantly bored

I buy three for a dollar
go inside the gas station
buy a bottle of water
thank the guy again on my way out
he's forgotten my existence
but says goodbye anyway
begin the walk back to the hotel

the distance doesn't seem as far
on the way back
it doesn't matter though
my mind is occupied
with a new task

as I walk I wash each of the Georgia peaches
carefully and thoroughly
with the water I bought
sniff the peaches in long deep breaths

As I approach the hotel I take
a small lick of the smallest peach
can't won't wait to get to the room
bite chew swallow

delicious and sublime

a bliss too important to experience
while walking toward the the setting sun
instead I order the sunset

to come to me
meet me right here
where I'm at
a command performance

I sit on the edge of the
hotel parking lot
sit on a concrete stopper
begin to eat the first peach
deliberately carefully

a blue car pulls up
slows down stops
window rolls down
two men peer down
you ok honey
the driver asks

yeah you ok there hun
the passenger asks
just sitting here enjoying my Georgia
peach
I say wanted to sit here and do nothing
else
but taste it

ok says the driver I get it
he nods as he puts the car in gear
well I sure as hell don't
the passenger says
but they drive away anyway

I'm one bite into the second Georgia
peach

when a hotel security guy in a little golf
cart drives up to me
hey you all right he asks
everything ok here
yeah I say holding up a Georgia peach in
each hand

I walked over to the gas station and
bought
a few peaches and decided
to eat them right here I say
he nods without smiling
the gas station he asks
yeah I answer that gas station and turn
my torso

I try to point but I have peaches in each
hand

so I gesture with both pieces of fruit
over there there's a guy selling them out front
the security guy doesn't say anything
just drives away
toward the gas station

I sit in Alabama with a Georgia peach
in each hand
a nibble here and there
making it last
daylight dwindles slowly
night emerges from the edges
accompanied by the
distant hum of the highway

I don't think about anything else except
eating my peaches
in the casino parking lot
by myself at sunset

I pretend I'm taking bites of the golden
sun as it sets in the sky
and the sun is kind enough to wait
until I finish both Georgia peaches
before it says goodnight

adornment

I catch a glimpse of myself in the mirror. I look like hell, and I know it. I'm wearing my denim capris, which are baggy at the bum and a skitch too tight at the waist. The hem, which hits at a funky spot on my leg, flares a bit more than what I'd like.

And the shirt. That shirt. Can't forget the shirt. It's a men's white and blue striped t-shirt from Target. No shape and boxy, too.

As for everything else? No jewelry, no makeup. My hair is doing the crazy cowlick thing again. I couldn't find my ballet flats, so I'm wearing my gym shoes: clunky, supportive, cushion-y and black. No socks.

And I just realized: my fly is open.

But I don't care. About any of it. I'm back home from the emergency room - I have strep throat, and my fever spiked to 104.5. Guess who's found out by accident that she's allergic to penicillin? Yeah, you know who.

I catch my reflection in the window, as I make my way up the front steps.
I look like hell.

All of it registers. And none of it matters.

Because when I wake up the next morning, I'm going to feel a tiny bit better. And, maybe by the end of the afternoon, I'll feel a fraction of a percent better that that.

And by the day after tomorrow rolls around. I'm going to be on the mend. I'll still feel sick, but I'll be almost myself again.

And that's will be the time to dig around for my favorite jeans, dark wash ones that flare perfectly. And I'll scare up my favorite Marc by Marc Jacobs flats…the red ones with the tiny mouse on each toe box. The ones that make me smile. Every. Single. Time. I. Wear. Them. I'll dig in my closet and find my super fuzzy and comfy black cashmere turtleneck sweater. The sleeves are just a touch too long, just the way I like it. Perfect for snuggling up on the couch.

I'll put on some cherry cola tinted lip balm, the one I've worn since high school, because it makes me feel pretty, and maybe spritz a tiny amount of my favorite perfume on my wrists.

I'll find those cashmere socks I got from a Christmas gift exchange a few years ago, the gray ones, with black polka dots at the toes.

Then, I'll brush my hair, and put a little bobby pin on the side. The white sparkly one, not the blue matte one. I'll want a little sparkly.

Then, I'll grab a book, and take the tea my husband will have made for me. I'll nestle into the couch, and put my feet up on the coffee table.

After a while, I'll start to doze off, curled up like a bean on the couch. Eventually, the phone will ring, and I'll dozily hear my husband answer and begin talking to my mom. She'll want to know how I'm feeling. Through sleepy eyes, I'll see him tiptoe over to check on me, then whisper into the phone: "She's wearing her black turtleneck....I think she's starting to feel better".

Wear what makes you feel better, and....well, you'll feel better. Whatever it is, and however you wear it is up to you.

You'll send that message out to the world.

That, while you're not always at the top of your game, you're going to be just fine.

time

I hit the snooze button three times. I shrugged the comforter off of my shoulders and reached for my cell phone. I swiped across the screen to look at the day's calendar: a doctor's appointment, a conference call, the middle school's open house, a mentoring appointment I couldn't postpone because I'd already canceled twice. I'd forgotten to pay the electric bill, so I would have to drop off the payment at the office, instead of paying online.

I wasn't even out of bed yet, and I was already exhausted.

My day was displaying in front of me, in no uncertain terms:

You don't have time.

I wanted to run to the gym to get a quick workout.

You don't have time.

I wanted to do some writing this afternoon.

You don't have time.

I put myself on auto-pilot. I forced myself to go to the gym, to an earlier class. Went to the class, worked out for half of the class, but had to leave early. *You don't have time.* Went home, took a shower, then grabbed my pen and journal. *You don't have time.* Drove to a park near the doctor's office, sat at a picnic table and wrote for 30 minutes.

You don't have time.

Paid the electric bill on the way to the mentoring session.
You don't have time.
Listened, helped, supported and mentored a friend starting a new business.
You don't have time.

Listened to the conference call in the car, on the way home. Participated just enough so the other callers thought I was paying attention.
You don't have time.
Arrived at home, supervised and helped while the kids did homework.
You don't have time.

Made dinner, started the dishes, then left for the school's open house.
You don't have time.
Attended open house, asked the appropriate questions, spoke with the teachers, chatted with the principal.
You don't have time.

Came home, signed forms, supervised bath time, bedtime, silly time, reading time, cuddle time.
You don't have time.
Turns out I did have time. Because you make the time for things which are the most important.

Remember what's most important in your day. And remember to put yourself in it.

You don't have time to do the things you don't want to to do. But you do have time for what matters.

Take the time.

food

Don't eat it, or you'll get fat. Eat it, you only live once. You shouldn't. You should. Be a sinner. Be a saint. Consume. Abstain.

I'm standing in the magazine section of Barnes & Noble. The sweet spot between the Women's section and the Food section. The gulf between indulge and and restraint. I'm asked to pick a side. Demanded, actually.

Both sides tell me I'll achieve the same thing: if I cook and eat, I will find a man. Keep a man. Make my children happy. Make friends and family like me. People will probably be jealous. But not too much cooking and eating...if I show restraint, I will look beautiful. I'll find a man, and keep him. I'll look like I'm 19 forever. I'll live forever. People will appreciate how much I care about them. People will probably be jealous.

I grab a stack of each, take them to the counter and pay. I go home with a tower of magazines and snuggle up on the couch.

I begin to read.

Whoever I am, according to these magazines, I'm doing it wrong. I'm not enough. But they'll fix me. And everyone will love me. Envy me. Want to be me.

My comfort or happiness or health is never discussed, unless it is to scare me. I should be scared. Everything I think is harmful, dangerous, outdated. But I can be fixed. Let the magazines fix me.

I should want to be fixed.

The pictures are pretty, though. Who wouldn't want to live in those pages? If I listen, I can be exactly like the people on the pages. Even happier, maybe.

I put down the magazines, and head to the kitchen. It's time to make dinner.

Who I am has nothing to do with the above archetypes. I want to be fed, without gorging. I want to be healthy without being sanctimonious.

I want to share my repast with my friends; whether we're splitting a cherry cola and a bag of Skittles, or dining in a 5-star tantalizing feast for all the senses.

Food is fuel and food is beauty. Comfort, love, happiness and energy on a plate.

I don't want to be made to feel guilty for any part of this process.

I want to be fed. I want to be present when others are fed.

But I'm not going to swallow everything that's being fed to me.

Neither should you.

www.ingramcontent.com/pod-product-compliance
Lightning Source LLC
Chambersburg PA
CBHW061449040426
42450CB00007B/1285